Awful, Disgusting Parasites

HEAD LICE

MARGARET MINCKS

BLACK
RABBIT
BOOKS

Bolt is published by Black Rabbit Books
P.O. Box 3263, Mankato, Minnesota, 56002.
www.blackrabbitbooks.com
Copyright © 2017 Black Rabbit Books

Design and Production by Michael Sellner
Photo Research by Rhonda Milbrett

Library of Congress Control Number: 2015954927

HC ISBN: 978-1-68072-007-5   PB ISBN: 978-1-68072-271-0

Printed in the United States at CG Book Printers,
North Mankato, Minnesota, 56003. PO #1792 4/16

Contents

CHAPTER 1

Meet
the Head Lice

Lice creep and crawl on a person's head. They bite down for a meal of blood. Then they quickly spread from person to person.

Lice are **parasites**. They live and feed on humans. These bloodsuckers are small and flat. They are hard to spot.

5

ANTENNAE

HEAD

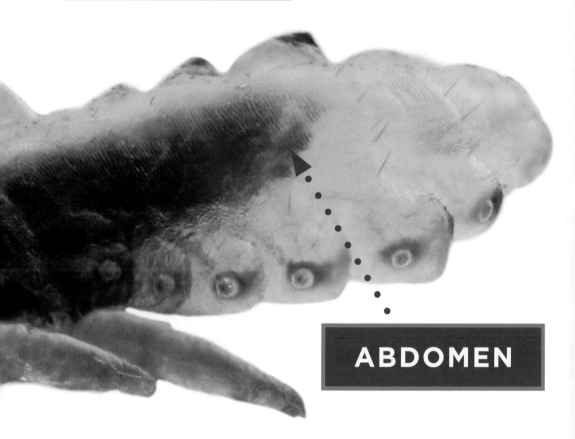

THORAX

ABDOMEN

CLAWS

7

CHAPTER 2

Tricky Travelers

Head lice do not fly or hop. They crawl. Claws help them hang onto hair. Lice also move fast and avoid light.

Head lice crawl from person to person when heads touch. Heads touch during hugs. Sharing a screen can also bring heads together.

· ·

As lice eat and grow, they change colors.

BIG
NUMBERS

MILLIONS OF KIDS   0   2   4

Anyone Can Get Lice

Getting head lice doesn't mean a person is dirty. Head lice are not picky. They will live on clean or dirty hair. Young kids are most likely to get head lice.

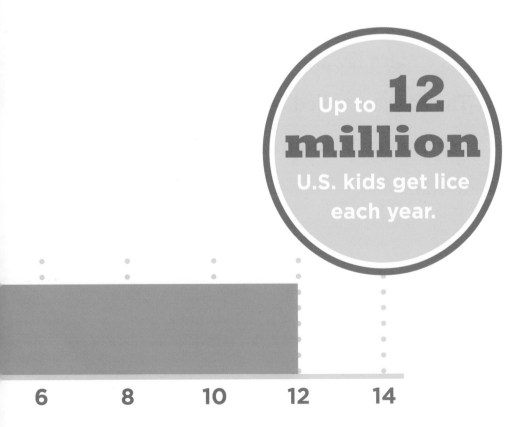

Up to **12 million** U.S. kids get lice each year.

6   8   10   12   14

CHAPTER 3

The Life of a Louse

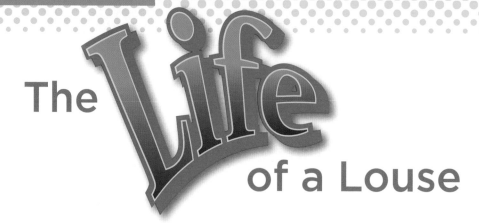

Head lice have three life stages. They start as eggs. Then they grow into **nymphs** and then into adults.

Females lay about six eggs a day. The eggs are called nits. Females use a sticky liquid to glue nits to hair.

ADULT

Ten days after hatching, an adult female begins to reproduce. It will lay between 50 and 150 eggs over the next 20 days.

EGG

An egg, called a nit, is glued to the hair where it stays for 6 to 9 days.

NYMPH

The nymph hatches. Then it sheds its outer covering three times in 10 days.

15

From Nymphs to Adults

Nits hatch in about a week. The young lice are called nymphs.

Nymphs shed their **exoskeletons** three times as they grow. Then they are adults.

Adult lice drink blood many times a day. They can live up to 30 days on a person's head.

Growing Up

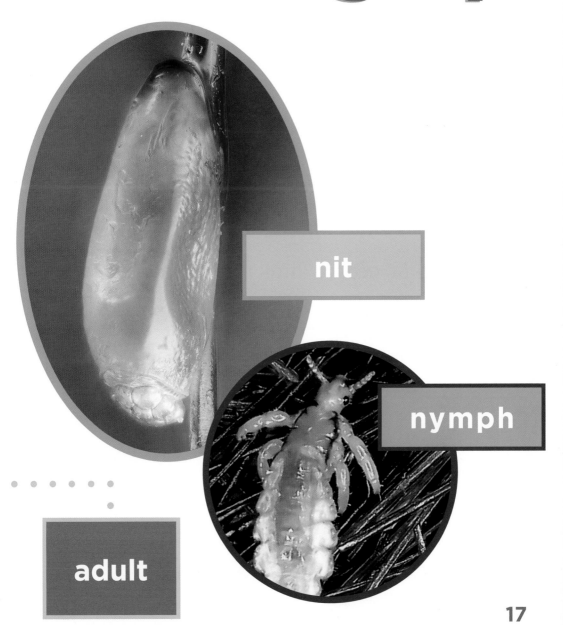

nit

nymph

adult

CHAPTER 4

Stopping Head Lice

It's hard to tell if someone has head lice. Some people get itchy **rashes**. However, head lice don't cause serious illness.

Some people think pets can spread these pests. But dogs, cats, and other pets cannot carry head lice.

Head lice can live on
eyelashes and eyebrows.

Symptoms

Head lice are most active in the dark. At bedtime, people might feel lice moving in their hair. The movement can make it hard to sleep.

SORES ON THE HEAD FROM SCRATCHING

Getting Lice Out

Lice and nits hide in hair. Using a comb to pull lice out works best. Some **medicated** shampoos can kill them.

There are ways to avoid getting lice. Stay away from people who have them. Keep hair tied back when sharing screens.

A HIGH PRICE

$100 $200

$50

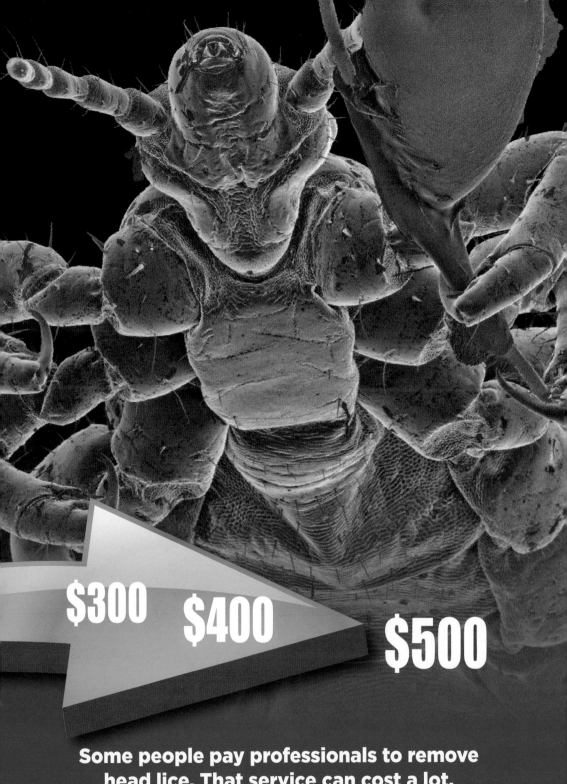

$300 **$400** **$500**

Some people pay professionals to remove
head lice. That service can cost a lot.

By the Numbers

.09 INCH
(2.3 MILLIMETERS)

average length of a louse

1 TO 2
days a head louse can survive without blood

average number
of nits a female lays
in a lifetime

88

Lice Lessons

Head lice are tricky. They make their homes on any person's head. Stay alert for these pests. And don't let the head lice bite.

Body lice are different from head lice. Body lice spread disease.

Helpful

Head Lice?

Scientists found head lice on
mummies in Peru. The mummies are
about 1,000 years old. The scientists
were surprised to find the lice weren't
the kinds they expected. Scientists
think studying the lice can help them
learn where ancient people
came from. Could these itchy
parasites really be helpful?

exoskeleton (ek-so-SKE-le-ten)—the hard, protective cover on the outside of an insect's body

louse (LAHWS)—a small, wingless insect that lives on people or animals; the plural of louse is lice.

medicated (med-uh-KAY-tid)—a product or item that contains medicine

nymph (NIMPF)—a young insect that has almost the same form as the adult

parasite (PAR-uh-syt)—a plant or animal that lives in or on another plant or animal and gets its food or protection from it

rash (RASH)—a group of red spots on the skin

BOOKS

Bugs: Facts at Your Fingertips. DK Pocket Genius. New York: DK Pub., 2012.

Gravel, Elise. *Head Lice.* Disgusting Creatures. Plattsburgh, NY: Tundra Books of Northern New York, 2015.

Shannon, David. *Bugs in My Hair!* New York: Blue Sky Press, 2013.

WEBSITES

Head Lice
www.kidshealth.org/parent/infections/common/head_lice.html

HeadLice.Org for Kids
www.headlice.org/kids/index.htm

Lice
www.pestworldforkids.org/pest-guide/lice/

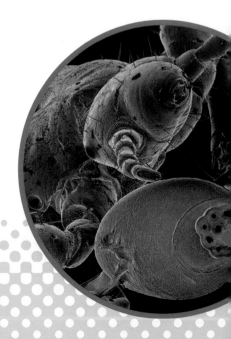